LETTER OF THANKS

I would like to thank my husband John and my children for their support. I also would like to thank Terrie Macklin, my best friend, partner and sister in the Gospel for typing for me. Thanks for your prayers, your time, and for believing in me. And thank you for your financial support even when I thought it was not possible. Thank you Yvonne Turner-Singh, my best friend, my sister and partner. Thanks for your support and all the cards you have sent to me to lift me up. Thank you again for your financial support and your sacrifice. I also would like to thank Sonia Papadopoulou for typing the poems for me. Thank you Kyle Lynch for saying yes, and for allowing God to use you at this time. Thanks for your humility. Thank you for being the illustrator of this book. Your words of support have really blessed me.

Karen Jackson

© Copyright 2008, Karen Jackson

All Rights Reserved.

No part of this book may be reproduced, stored in
a retrieval system, or transmitted by any means,
electronic, mechanical, photocopying, recording,
or otherwise, without written permission
from the author.

ISBN: 978-1-60414-107-8

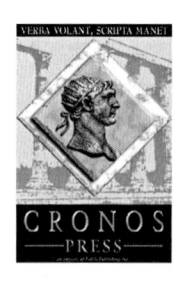

DEDICATION

This book is dedicated to my Lord and Savior Jesus Christ. Who is the head of my life. It was the Holy Spirit who inspired me to write these words. For people to meditate and receive a closer walk with God and to feel comforted as it begins to melt away whatever is or should not be in their life.

"Poems to live by" are words that rhyme with rhythm with God as He (God) so personally begins to minister to your heart, soul and mind. To make you feel you are with Him (God) all the time.

Karen Jackson

INTRODUCTION

I am a wife and mother of three children, Pamela, Lamont and John John. And I'm a grandmother of three, Tyrone, Tim, and Regine. I'm also an ordain minister of the Gospel of Jesus Christ. As an ordain minister, I have conducted seminars to inspire women and held workshops and given encouraging messages through my tape ministry. I'm a native of New York City where I lived most of my adult life. I recently relocated to South Carolina and I attend Redemption World Outreach Center.

Karen Jackson

A NEW DAY

THE LAST YEAR HAS PASSED AWAY
MAY THIS NEW YEAR
BRING BLESSINGS AND
HAPPINESS YOUR WAY,
AND STAY FOREVER
AND A DAY.

Karen Jackson

Morning Joy

I just want to say
What you mean to me today
Throughout the years, of you
Prayers and tears.
It has brought me through
All of my fears
That's why I'm here for you
Today in everyway.

Karen Jackson

GOD'S LIGHT

MAY THIS DAY THAT THE LORD HAS MADE
BE THE BEST DAY OF YOUR LIFE,
YOU ARE GOD'S DELIGHT
YOU ARE HIS BEST IN HIS SIGHT,
PRECIOUS ONE WHEN YOU WALK AND TALK
YOU BRING GOD'S GLORIOUS LIGHT, SO WONDERFUL
AND BRIGHT,
MAY ALL THE DAYS OF YOUR LIFE BE FILLED
WITH HIS MARVELOUS LIGHT.

Karen Jackson

Morning

Showers of flowers raining
On the earth
To bring a
New birth to the earth

Rainbow of colors
Red, yellow, white
And pink-all to
Restore so that my
People will live forever more
And no more to be poor.
Now open the door
And allow
Me to come in and live- in you
For I AM the door
The truth and the light
I want to shine bright
In your sight.

Karen Jackson

Look

Look over the horizon and
arise from your **Rest**

Look at the sunset and know
that you're **Set**

Look at the bright and morning **Star**
and know that you **Are**

Look at the fields and know that
you are **Real**

Now look at your future and
know that this is the real **Picture.**

Karen Jackson

HIS PRESENCE

THERE ARE LEAVES BLOWING IN THE WIND
COME AND HEAR HIS VOICE WHISPERING IN OUR EAR
AS WE FEEL HIS PRESENCE, I SENSE HIM VERY NEAR
THERE IS NO NEED TO FEAR
FOR GOD IS LOVE
HE IS AS GENTLE AS A DOVE,
OUR HEAVENLY FATHER IS FROM ABOVE.

Karen Jackson

"THERE IS A PLACE"

EVEN THOUGH YOUR LIFE MAY SEEMED TO BE AT A STAND STILL.
KNOW THAT HE IS THERE
THOUGH YOUR WATERS MIGHT HAVE BEEN MUDDY
KNOW THAT A DROP OF HIS WORD
ALL SHALL BE CLEAR
SO MY DEAR NEVER FEAR
BECAUSE HE'S ALWAYS BEEN THERE
NEVER BE IN DOUBT, JUST KNOW
WITHOUT A DOUBT, HE WILL ALWAYS BRING YOU OUT.
SO COME TO A PLACE IN YOUR MIND
AND YOU WILL FIND
THAT GOD IS DEVINE.

Karen Jackson

"The water of life"

As the rain comes down from Heaven
and drop on the leaves of the tree
surely I believe…
God will water the garden
of my heart
knowing that I will never
be dry but be alive
Dishing the water of life
from the fountain of God
so look alive
knowing God will surely water
your garden, and you will not be forgotten
but be remembered in God's
Heaven.

Karen Jackson

"I'LL GO TO THE MOUNTAIN"

I'LL GO TO THE MOUNTAIN AND THERE
I'LL RECEIVE MY LORD…
I'LL GO TO THE MOUNTAIN OF SALVATION
AND RECEIVE MY CONSOLATION.
NOW I'M FREE
OH NOW I'M FREE
I CAN CLEARLY SEE
MY DESTINATION

I'VE BEEN TO THE MOUNTAIN
I'VE BEEN TO THE FOUNTAIN
HE IS MY ROCK
HE IS MY WATER
BECAUSE OF THAT I DRAW FOREVER.
I'LL ALWAYS REMEMBER,
HE IS MY HELP IN A TIME OF NEED
AND BECAUSE OF THAT I BOW MY KNEE,
NOW AND FOREVER, MY WONDERFUL SAVIOR.

Karen Jackson

"UNDER A TREE"

I'M SWINGING UNDER A TREE
LOOKING TO WHAT I CAN SEE,
JUST MY SWING AND ME
THE SUN IS SHINNING SO BRIGHT
WHAT A DELIGHT, IT IS FOR ME TO SEE,

THE CLOUDS SO HIGH IN THE SKY
JUST WATCHING THEM GO BY
AND GRASS TICKLING ME AND MAKING ME LAUGH,
LOOKING OVER AND SEEING THE WATER SO CLEAR
IT MAKES ME WANT TO DRAW NEAR,

AND HEAR THE WATER BEATING ON THE ROCKS
SOUNDING LIKE MY MOTHERS KNOCK
I MUST GO NOW! I HEAR MY MOTHER CALLING
VERY LOUD
BUT TOMORROW I'LL BE HERE AGAIN
SWINGING UNDER THE TREE,
MY SWING AND ME.

Karen Jackson

Please...

Please will you allow me
to come in and have some peace

Please won't you allow me to be free
and just be me

Please can I bring my friend to
play with me

Please can I write what I see

Please can I explore
and bring more
so the people won't be poor

Please may I speak what's on
my mind, and share what's in my heart,
without you throwing darts.

Please can I love
That's were it came from above

Please let people have a chance to see eye to eye
Please...

Karen Jackson

"I'm Here"

I'm here though I'm full of fear
I'm here and things has fallen all around me,
I'm so afraid
Even though I can hear
I don't know where to go from here
Where do I go?
Do I stay here?
Or go there?
I think I need to stay here,
So that I can hear
With my ear (heart)
And not be in fear
Now fear is know longer here-
God has not given me a spirit of fear, but of love and power
and a sound mind.

Karen Jackson

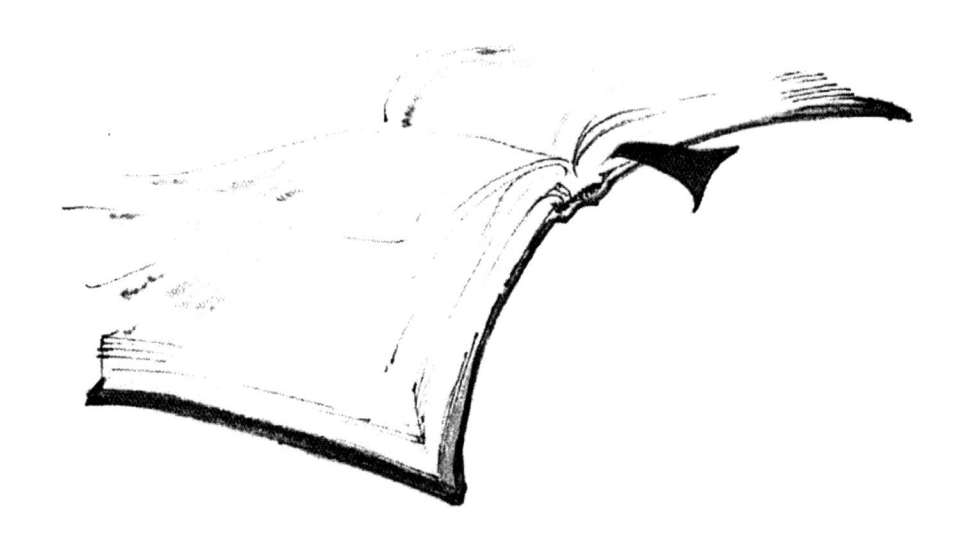

SET FREE

*THANK YOU LORD THAT I'M FREE
FROM ALL OF MY INFIRMITIES
THANK YOU LORD FOR THE WORD,
THAT YOU IMPARTED TO ME
THANK YOU LORD FOR THE WORD OF LIFE,
THAT SETS US FREE FROM ALL OF OUR ANXIETIES.*

Karen Jackson

THE GIVER OF LIVE

*THANK YOU LORD, THANK YOU LORD, FOR GIVING US LIFE
THANK YOU LORD, THANK YOU LORD,
THAT YOU GAVE US,
YOUR BODY.
THANK YOU LORD, THANK YOU LORD, FOR BARING OUR
INFIRMITIES
SO THAT WE COULD BE FREE.
THANK YOU LORD, THANK YOU LORD, FOR SPILLING YOUR
BLOOD
OUTWARDLY, SO THAT WE COULD TAKE IT INWARDLY.
THE BLOOD THAT YOU OFFERED FOR US,
SO THAT WE COULD LIVE. THANK YOU LORD,
THANK YOU LORD, THAT WE HAVE ACCESS TO THE TREE
OF LIFE, BECAUSE YOU ARE THE GIVER OF LIFE.*

Karen Jackson

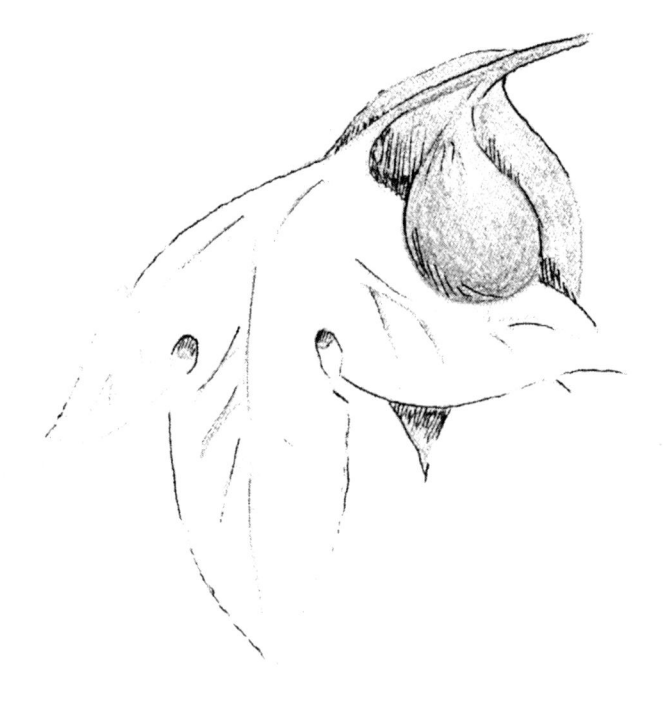

SWADDLE

S IN CAME AFTER ADAM ATE THE FRUIT

W ITH THE BLOOD OF JESUS,
HE RANSOMED US BACK

A GAIN, NOT TO

D IE BUT TO LIVE A

D EVINE

L IFE WITH HIM FOR

E TERNITY

Karen Jackson

Poems to Live By

AGAPE

A FTER THE SON OF

G OD

A PPEARED TO MARY MAGDALENE, HE

P RESENTED HIS PRECIOUS BLOOD TO THE FATHER
SO THAT WE COULD LIVE WITH HIM FOR

E TERNITY.

Karen Jackson

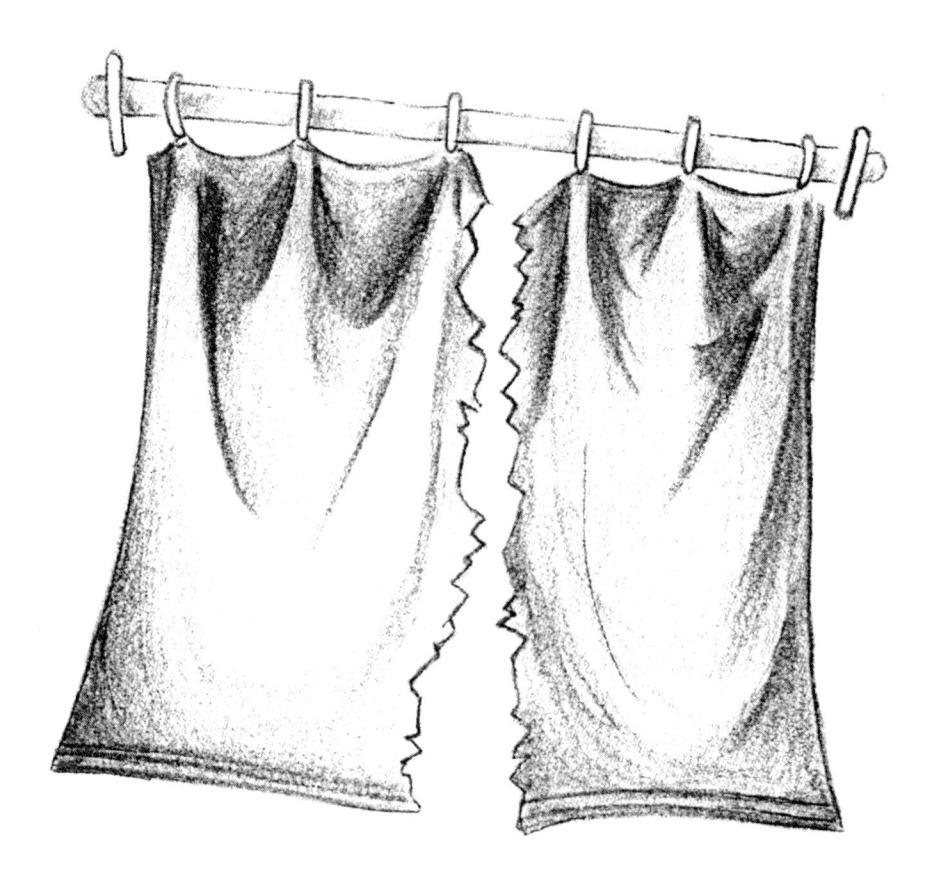

ACCESS TO THE THRONE

WE WILL NOT FAIL
WE WILL PREVAIL,
BECAUSE OF THE VEIL
THAT HE RIPPED INTO

SO THAT WE COULD COME TO YOU,
BOLDLY TO YOUR THRONE OF GRACE
AND RECEIVE YOUR FAITH,

YOU ARE SO SWEET AND SO KIND
SO GLAD YOU STAY ON MY MIND,
ALL THE TIME

I WILL STAY IN YOUR VINE,
BECAUSE YOU ARE MINE
SO DEAR AND SO FINE,
I WILL ALWAYS BE THINE.

Karen Jackson

FROM WHOM ALL BLESSING FLOW

THANK YOU LORD FOR THE EVERLASTING WATERS

THAT FOREVER RISES UP IN ME, THANK YOU LORD,

FOR THE SPIRIT OF LIFE, THAT LIVETH IN ME

THANK YOU FATHER FOR THE BLOOD THAT SET ME

FREE, FROM ALL OF MY INFIRMITIES.

Karen Jackson

LOVE

L IFE CAME

O UT OF THE FATHER FOR US TO HAVE

V ICTORY OVER THE DEVIL FOR

E TERNITY

Karen Jackson

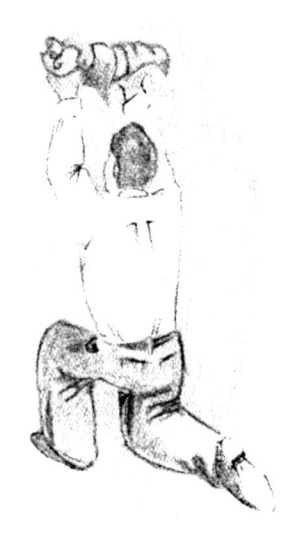

GIVE

G   OD FIRST GAVE HIS SON AS AN OFFERING FOR US TO GIVE

I   NTO THE KINGDOM AND REVERSING THE CURSE HAVING

V   ICTORY OVER THE DEVIL FOR

E   TERNITY LIVING IN COMPLETE LIFE NOW AND FOREVER.

Karen Jackson

"THAT WONDERFUL NAME"

I CALL ON THAT WONDERFUL NAME,
BECAUSE I'M NOT ASHAMED
OH JESUS, OH JESUS
HE BROUGHT ME FROM SHAME,
HE SAID THERE IS NO BLAME
OH! JESUS, OH! JESUS
THE MAN THAT DIED FOR ME
ON THAT RUGGED TREE
WHERE HE CARRIED MY INFIRMITIES
HE TOOK MY SIN AND SHAME,
HE SAID I'LL NEVER BE THE SAME
OH! JESUS, OH! JESUS
HE WILL NEVER CHANGE
HE IS THE SAME
THE MAN WHO BROUGHT ME FROM SIN AND SHAME
OH! JESUS, OH! JESUS

Karen Jackson

TRUTH

IT HAS ALWAYS BEEN SAID
EVEN FROM THE MEN THAT ARE DEAD,
THAT TRUTH WILL MAKE YOU FREE,
SO YOU SEE THAT TRUTH CAME FROM THE
SEED OF GOD.

THE TRUTH THAT CAN NEVER DIE,
THE TRUTH THAT CAN NEVER LIE.

THAT TRUTH THAT CAN LIVE THROUGH
YOUR MORTAL BODY.

THAT TRUTH THAT WILL BRING LIFE TO YOU.

A TRUTH THAT IS AND WILL ALWAYS BE,
NOW AND FOREVER, TRUTH CAME FROM THE
FATHER OF LIGHTS
NOW YOU SEE, WHEN YOU GET THE TRUTH,
NOT ONLY WILL IT SET YOU FREE,
IT WILL LIGHTEN UP YOUR VERY BEING
SO THAT MAN CAN SEE ME, JESUS.

Karen Jackson

MIRACLE

M AN

I S

R ISEN BECAUSE

A FTER THE FALL OF ADAM

C HRIST JESUS CAME AND BESTOWED

L IFE FOR US TO LIVE NOW AND FOREVER AND

E TERNITY WITH GOD.

Karen Jackson

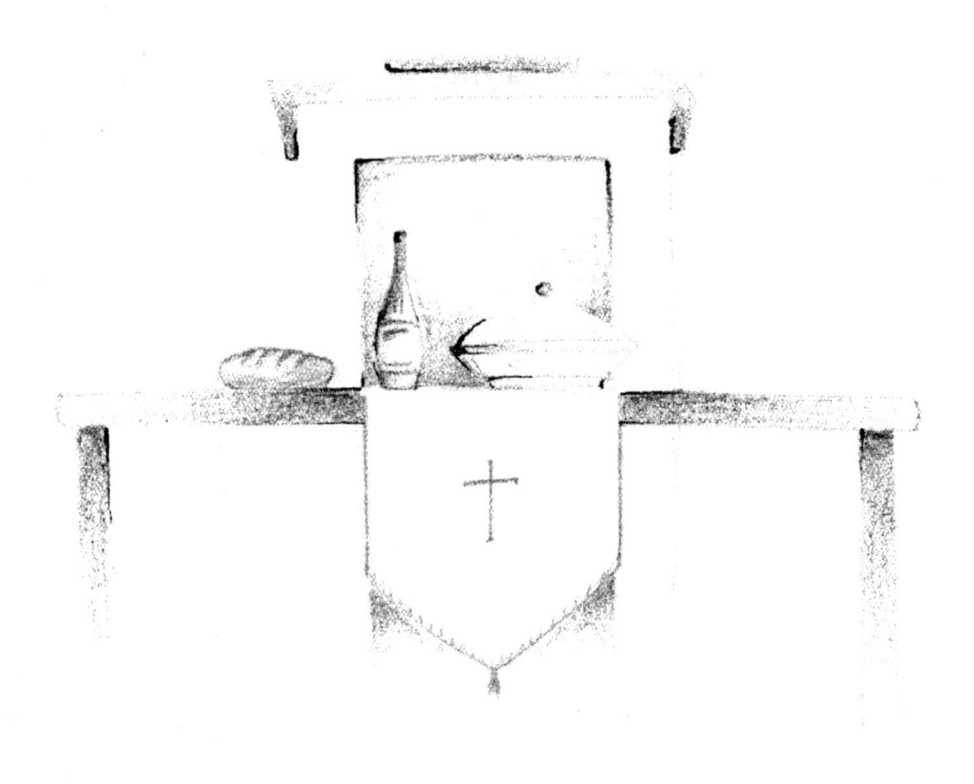

FEAST

F ATHER WE WILL

E AT

A FTER YOU

S UPPER YOU HAVE GIVEN US

T AKE EAT THIS IS MY BODY BROKEN FOR YOU.

Karen Jackson

JACK AND THE SEED

DEAR SIR WOULD YOU BUY MY COW
SO MY MOTHER AND I COULD HAVE SOME CHOW?
AND THE MAN REPLIED, "SILVER AND GOLD, HAVE I NONE
BUT I HAVE SEED FOR YOU TO SOW,
SO THAT YOU WOULD KNOW HOW TO LIVE"
AND JACK REPLIED, "THANK YOU SIR,
I WILL GO HOME AND PLANT THESE SEEDS IN GOOD SOIL,
AND TAKE BACK THE SPOIL THAT THE DEVIL HAD TAKEN
FROM ME
FOR GREATER IS HE THAT IS IN ME
AND NOR WILL I EVER LACK,
FOR WHEN I PLANT THE DEVIL HAS TO GET BACK
FOR MY NAME IS JACK,
NOR WILL I LACK IN ANY GOOD THING
I WILL BRING MY OFFERING PRAISING AND SINGING".

Karen Jackson

"Thanks Giving"

T he Father that
H as brought us out of darkness
A nd put us in
N ewness of life, and placed us in the
K ingdom of His dear
S on (Jesus)

G od has
I ntervene for us, and the
V eil was ripped into so that we could come
I n the presence of God
N ow and forever
G iving Him sacrifices of praise.

Karen Jackson

Joy

Christ Jesus is the true vine
We are the branches
When we drink from the
Grapevine of
Jesus
His Joy will cause our
Joy to be full.
Jesus became our joy
Because He overcame yesterday.

Karen Jackson

LIVE

L IFE CAME FROM WITH

I N THE

V INE FOR MAN TO

E AT AND LIVE

OH! LET THOSE WHO ARE CALLED DEAD LET
THEM LIVE

OH LIVE AND NOT DIE,
THE DEVIL JUST TOLD YOU A LIE.

LOOK IN MY EYES, AND YOU WILL SEE AGAIN
AND LIVE FOREVER, EVEN TILL THE END.

I AM HE THAT WAS DEAD
NOW I AM ALIVE FOREVER MORE.

WHOSOEVER IS IN THE VINE
ALL IS MINE,
WHAT IS MINE IS THINE
STAY IN THE VINE,
AND YOU WILL BE JUST FINE.

Karen Jackson

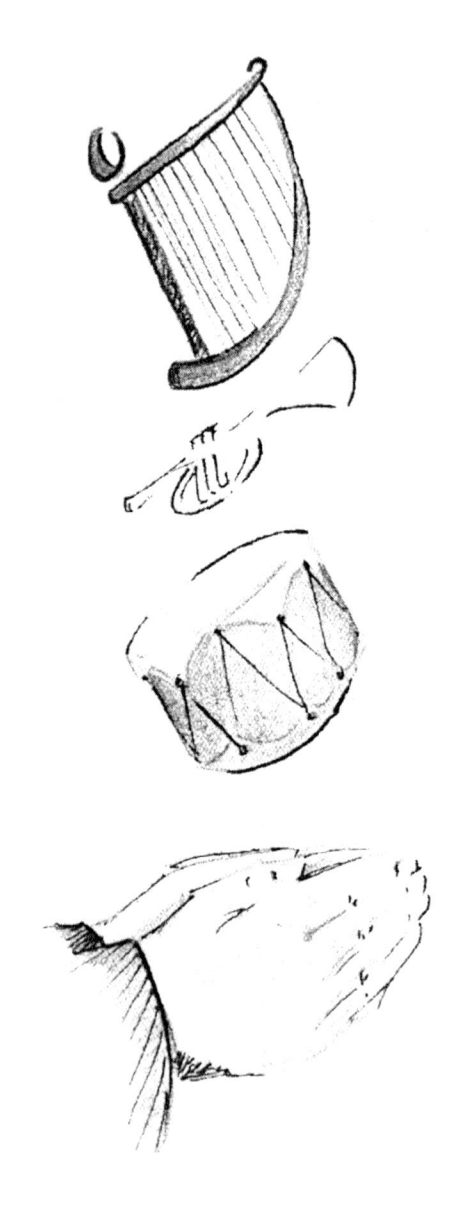

Poems to Live By

PSALMS

P RAISES

S HALL

A LWAYS BE PART OF MY

L IFE

M AGNIFYING MY

S AVIOR ALL THE DAY LONG

Karen Jackson

Blessed

Blessed is he that is poor,
For He Jesus
Will make him
Rich over all.

Karen Jackson

A Merry Heart

May your heart be
Happy and true
Remember I will
Always love you.

Karen Jackson

"TWO HEARTS"

TWO HEARTS MADE FOR EACH OTHER
YET DO NOT KNOW ONE ANOTHER.
WANT TO SEPARATE BUT THEY ANTICIPATE.
TWO HEARTS MADE FOR EACH OTHER,
EACH IN THEIR OWN SEPARATE WORLDS,

REACHING FOR THE UNREACHABLE
WANT TO RELATE BUT WON'T PARTICIPATE,
WANT TO REACH NOT WILLING TO STRETCH
TWO HEARTS THAT ARE BROKEN AND NEED MENDING,
BUT NEITHER WANTS TO SAY I'M SORRY

WAITING ON ONE ANOTHER TO SAY TO EACH OTHER,
YET NO WORDS COME
ONE NEEDS TO MEND.
YET NO ONE WANTS TO SEND
TWO HEARTS THAT ARE MEANT FOR ONE ANOTHER.

Karen Jackson

GOD'S GIFT

GOD GAVE US HIS GRACE
SO WE WOULD HAVE A PLACE
IN THE UNIVERSE
GOD GAVE US HIS GIFTS IN ORDER FOR US
TO BECOME FRUITFUL
GOD GAVE US HIS GOODNESS FOR US TO
LIVE GODLY
AND RECEIVE HIS GOODS

Karen Jackson

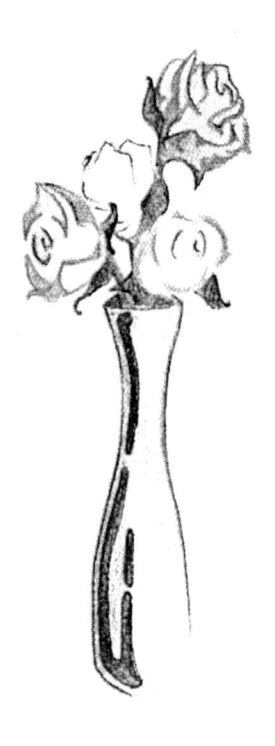

Mother's gift

Mother I give to you a pink rose, God's grace
Mother I give to you a yellow rose, God's friendship
Mother I give to you a white rose, God's purity
Mother I give to you a red rose, God's perfect love

Karen Jackson

THREE WOMEN IN WAITING...

THERE ARE WOMEN WAITING
AND THEY ARE MEDITATING
AND NOT HESITATING,
PRAYING AND STAYING IN GOD'S PRESENCE

Karen Jackson

MY BUTTERFLY

THERE WAS MARY, MARTHA
AND MIRIAM

AND THERE WERE OTHERS
BUT THERE IS ONLY ONE
MOTHER!

AND BESIDES YOU
THERE IS NONE OTHER.
AND THE OTHERS
JUST MAKE UP
MOTHER!

Karen Jackson

To The Women in the Body of Christ

For We Are
SPECIAL

S   weetness that God

P   erfected in our hearts for

E   veryone. And

C   onquering every endeavour

I   n every area of our lives.

A   ffecting lives we touch,

L   oving – Kindness from the God we serve.

Karen Jackson

THREE FOLD BLESSING

THREE BROTHERS
IN UNITY
BRINGING IT INTO THEIR
COMMUNITY.

Karen Jackson

TO MY FATHER

I WRITE THIS NOTE TO YOU
JUST TO SAY HOW MUCH I LOVE YOU,
I'M GLAD TO BE YOUR SON
YOU AND I HAVE SO MUCH FUN,
I PRAY YOU RECEIVE THE BEST
AS YOU ENTER INTO MY FATHER'S REST.
LOVE,
YOUR SON

Karen Jackson

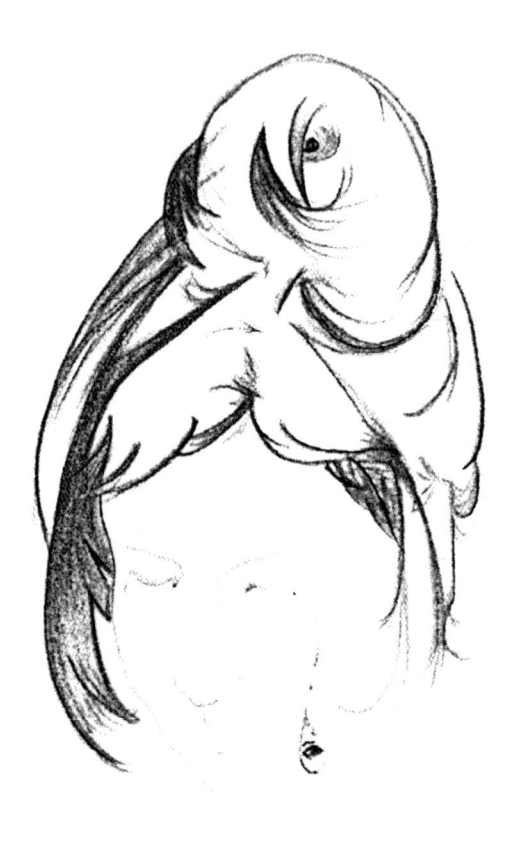

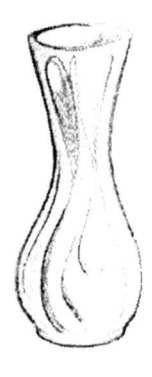

"THE WOMAN OF SORROW"

THE WOMAN OF SORROW SHE BELIEVES,
THERE WILL BE NO TOMORROW
FOR GOD SAY'S "WEEP NO MORE,
FOR I WILL RESTORE,
AND BRING YOU MORE,
THEN BEFORE."
YOU ARE BLESSED, I HAVE COME
TO GIVE YOU MY BEST.
LET YOUR SORROWS BE YOUR TOMORROWS
AND LOOK TO TODAY
FOR I AM HERE TO STAY
GOD'S EYE, IS ON YOUR TEARS
HAVE NO FEAR
FOR I THE LORD GOD I AM HERE.

Karen Jackson

Awaken

When I awaken to the morning sun
Where I left my tears upon my pillow
Where I was crying all night.
I could hear the rushing of the
Sea, it reminded me of my sorrow,
I was just wondering about my tomorrow,
If I could just capture a glimpse of peace.
And bring it into myself, where
My sea is rushing inside of me,
I could make it one more day,
And look over the clear horizon
Where my Savior has come to say
I AM here to stay.

Karen Jackson

My Cry

I sought the Lord and the Lord
Heard my cry-
Your cry wasn't loud
My daughter you have been found
when you spoke My words
They were clear and profound
it had that heavenly sound
that cause Me to stand still
and look around
and because of that
know that I can be found
I AM your God
And your Savior
And know you're always have favor
Continue my daughter praying fervently
Know you're always be with me for eternity.

Karen Jackson

A LIGHT IN A WINDOW

THERE ARE TIMES WHEN WE HAVE DARK AND
GRAY AREAS IN OUR LIVES, AND WE NEED
SOMEONE TO BRING THAT LIGHT TO THAT
AREA,
GOD ALWAYS HAS THAT PERSON THERE TO
ILLUMINATE THE DARK AREA IN OUR LIFE,
AND BRING US INTO A PLACE IN GOD WITHIN
OURSELVES.
COME AND LET ME BRING THAT LIGHT,
I KNOW IS NIGHT…
LOOK AND SEE AND KNOW IT'S GOING TO BE
ALL RIGHT
FOR YOU ARE NOT OUT OF HIS SIGHT
YOU ARE PRECIOUS
YOU HAVE BEEN BOUGHT WITH HIS PRICE
SO COME AND LOOK AT THIS LIGHT
AND ALLOW ME TO BE YOUR LIGHT TONIGHT
LOOK UP I'LL ALWAYS BE THAT LIGHT IN THE
WINDOW.

Karen Jackson

"I'M COMING PASS"

I'M COMING PASS JUST TO SEE WHO WILL FAST
AND AS I LOOK AND SEE
JUST WHO WILL INTERCEDE FOR ME,
AND WHO WOULD PRAY AND FAST
ON MY BEHALF,
AS YOU SEE
I NEED SOMEONE TO INTERCEDE,
AND I WILL STOP THE BOW FROM THE ENEMY
BECAUSE HE IS A DEFEATED FOE,
AND YOU MUST KNOW
I WILL BRING HIM BELOW,
BECAUSE THAT IS WHERE HE MUST GO
SO BECAUSE OF THIS,
IT WILL NOT BE A BLISS
I AM WHAT I SAY I AM,
SO STAND FAST
I AM COMING FAST,
AND THEN AT LAST
I'LL KNOW LONGER BE IN THE PASS,
I AM THE FIRST AND THE LAST.

Karen Jackson

MY PRAYER

LORD AS I BRING THE PEOPLE BEFORE YOU
THE PEOPLE THAT SEEMINGLY TO BE BOUND,

OH! ONLY IF THEY WOULD JUST LOOK AROUND
THEY WOULD SEE THEIR ENEMY IS NO
WHERE TO BE
FOUND.

WHY ARE THE PEOPLE WEARING A FROWN?
YOUR WORD IS CLEAR AND PROFOUND,
WHEN THEY STAY IN YOUR WORD, THEY WILL
NEVER FALL TO THE GROUND,

LORD IF WE CONTINUE TO STAND ON HOLY
GROUND,
ONE DAY SOON WE WILL WEAR OUR CROWN.

Karen Jackson

WHERE THERE IS...

WHERE THERE IS GROSS DARKNESS,
THERE IS BRIGHTNESS AND RAYS OF LIGHT.

WHERE THERE ARE SCREAMS FROM THE DEEP
THERE ARE PRAISES FROM ABOVE.

WHERE THERE ARE WITCHES AND WARLOCKS,
THERE ARE KINGS AND PRIESTS.

WHERE THERE ARE SKELETONS AND SIGNS OF DEATH,
THERE IS LIFE AND SIGNS OF THE LIVING.

WHERE THERE ARE DEMONS AND DEMONIC FORCES,
THERE ARE CHERUBIMS AND ANGELS DESCENDING AND
ASCENDING FROM ON
HIGH.

WHERE THE DEVIL REIGNS,
THE LORD JESUS CHRIST HAS CONQUERED DEATH AND
HE SAID.

"LET THERE BE LIGHT
LET US CONTINUE TO WALK IN THE LIGHT
WHERE THERE IS LIGHT,
THERE IS LIFE.
THERE IS NO NEED TO FIGHT,
GOD HAS BROUGHT US TO HIS MARVELOUS LIGHT,
SO BRILLIANT AND BRIGHT.
WHERE THERE IS THE STAR
REST ASSURE GOD IS NOT FAR."

Karen Jackson

Come in

Come in from the storm
And wrap up in my arms
No need to fear,
Know that I'm here
Come from the cold
And just unfold
And let me tell you
A story that has
Never been told-
There is a Man
That knows all about
Your fears, and tears
Just let Him release
You from all of your
Fears.

Karen Jackson

THE SPIRIT OF POWER

BEFORE I LAY MY HEAD UPON MY PILLOW,
I WOULD LIKE FOR MY WORDS TO BECOME
SWEET AND MELLOW,
TO THE EAR OF THE FATHER
AS THE SPIRIT OF POWER,
HAS BOUGHT ME TO THIS
VERY HOUR,
I CAN'T HELP BUT REMEMBER
IT IS HE THAT HAS BOUGHT ME,
FROM HEAR TO ETERNITY
AND IT WILL BE HIM, THAT WILL BRING ME IN
AS I SING MY FAVORITE HYMN,
I WILL ALWAYS REMEMBER HE IS MY LORD AND SAVIOR.

Karen Jackson

HE IS THE FIRST AND LAST

GOING FORWARD FOR TOMORROW
FOR IN IT THERE IS NO SORROW,
PRESSING TOWARD THE MARK THAT
IS SET BEFORE YOU,
YOU'LL NEVER BE BLOCKED
FOR IT WAS SET BY THE MAKER,
HE IS OUR RECORD BREAKER
FOR HE IS OUR CREATOR,
HE IS THE BEGINNING AND OUR END
HE IS THE END OF THE BEGINNING,
HE IS THE FIRST AND THE LAST
AND IF WE HOLD FAST
WE'LL SEE IT COME TO PASS
AND SOON AT LAST
OUR END WILL BE IN THE PASS.

Karen Jackson

THE REVELATION OF PRAYER

P RAYING ALWAYS WITH ALL PRAYER AND SUPPLICATION IN THE SPIRIT FOR ALL SAINTS.

R ETURNING THE WORD THAT CAME

A FTER GOD ASCENDED FROM ON HIGH, KNOWING

Y OUR PRAYERS HAVE BEEN HEARD.

E RASING DOUBT FROM YOUR MIND BECAUSE NOTHING GOES UNHEARD WHEN IT,

R EACHES THE FATHER GOD.

Karen Jackson

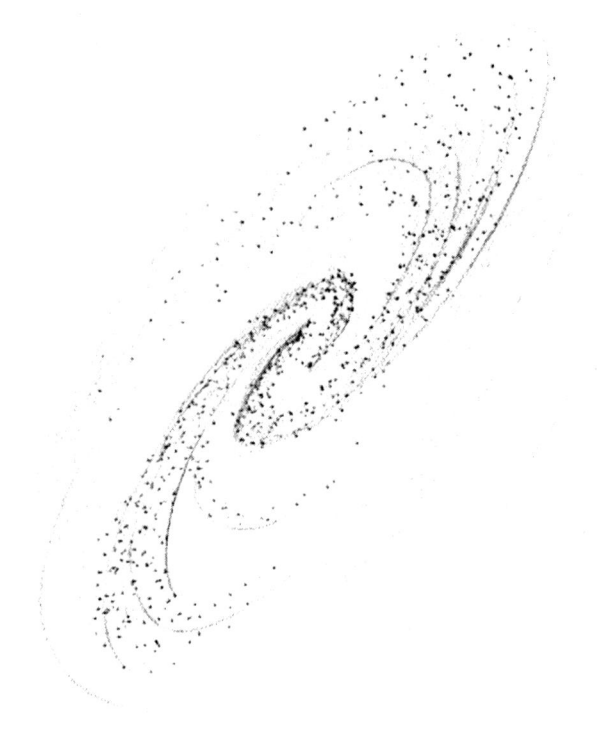

"A prayer of an endless day"

Today begins tomorrow
It begins – in knowing no end.
Even though we don't know
How it's going to begin
Let's talk about how it's going to end-
In knowing that God always
Starts everything in the end.
The end is the beginning of our end.
Now let's begin again- Lord thank you
That you have began my day today
In knowing this is my endless day.

Karen Jackson

Exodus Poem

All the kings horses
And all the kings men could not follow them-
And God put them to an end-
The sea swallow them
And they were not seen anymore
And the Israelites won the war
But, there is more
God does not want us poor
Be strong in spirit and in His might
stand still and let God fight.

Karen Jackson

Victory

When I know it's you I
can walk through-
and I'll never be blue,
because of you-
I can look to tomorrow
And know there is no sorrow
And yet I have know need
To borrow-
You became poor in your soul
So that we would become
rich in our spirit.

Karen Jackson

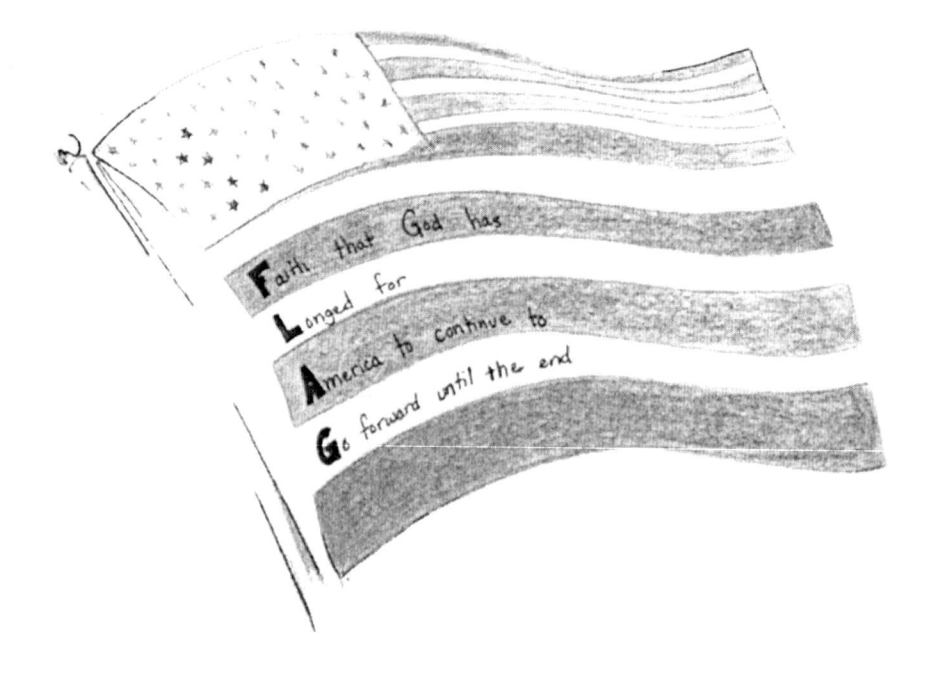

Faith that God has
Longed for
America to continue to
Go forward until the end

FLAG

F AITH THAT GOD HAS

L ONGED FOR

A MERICA TO CONTINUE TO

G O FORWARD UNTIL THE END.

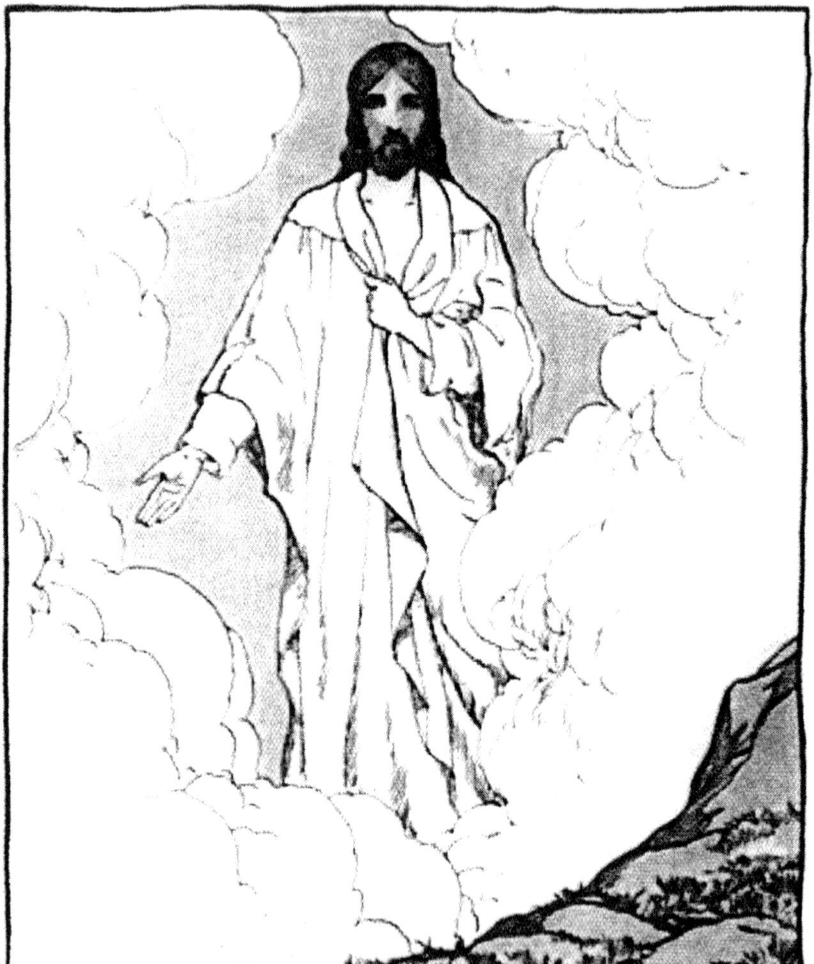

SOON TO APPEAR

NOW AS I LAY MY HEAD TO REST
I KNOW LORD YOU WANT US TO
HAVE THE VERY BEST

IT HAS NOT YET APPEARED
NOR HAS IT ENTERED INTO OUR EAR
WHAT YOU WOULD WANT US TO HEAR

WE KNOW WE ARE VERY NEAR
YOU WILL SOON APPEAR
AND ALL YOUR PEOPLE WILL SOON BE
FREE FROM ALL FEAR

AS WE DRAW NEAR
OH! FATHER WE LOOK FORWARD TO HEAR
YOUR VOICE IN OUR EAR AT THAT HOUR.

Karen Jackson

Jesus Is Risen

**Jesus Christ
Has Risen,
To give us
His Life!**

Karen Jackson

Poems to Live By

LIFE FOREVER

L OOKING UNTO JESUS WHICH

I S THE AUTHOR AND FINISHER OF OUR

F AITH

E NDURING THE RACE THAT GOD HAS SET BEFORE US.

Karen Jackson

Christmas

*Though Christmas
is near*

*Some of us will have
happiness some
will have fear*

*Some will come far
and some near,*

*Whether you are here
or there,*

*Know for sure
that Christ*

*Can be your
Christmas.*

Karen Jackson

JESUS

J ESUS

E VER LASTING

S AVIOR

U NTO US A

S ON WAS GIVEN

Karen Jackson

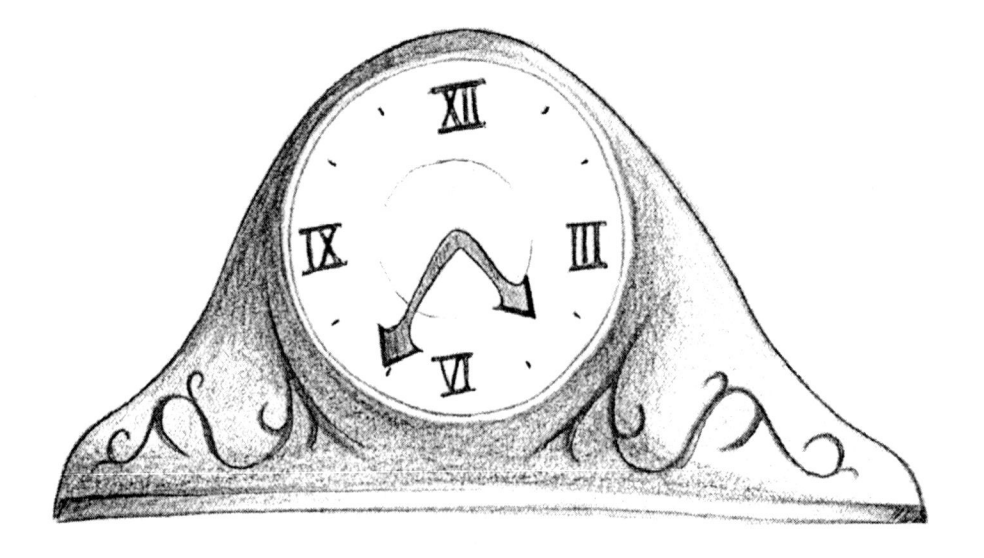

God's clock

At one o'clock-we're going to have fun with the Son.
At two o'clock- we're going threw to be with Bro Drew
At three o'clock- it's soon going to be time for Bebee to knock at the door
At four o'clock-we then will open the door for the poor
At five o'clock-we will divide our spoil and share our oil.
At six o'clock -We will mix our ingredients of faith
At seven o'clock-we'll prepare ourselves to reach heaven
At eight o'clock- then we'll know, we'll not be late, for that open gate
At nine o'clock-then God will dine with us
At ten o'clock-because then it'll be time for the hour eleven o'clock-we'll all be in heaven
At twelve o'clock-all is well, prepare yourself for the hour is approaching. Don't be late, be at that pearly gate. And of course began at one so that you'll be with the Son.

Karen Jackson

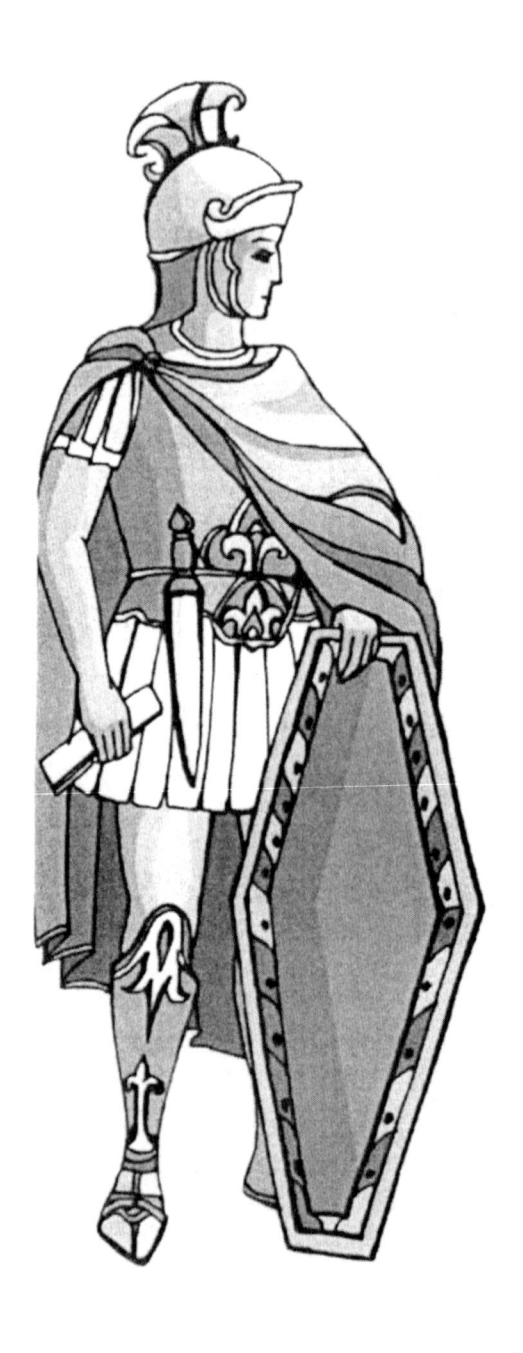

WRAPPED IN GOD

WHEN YOU ARE WRAPPED
WITH THE WRAPPINGS OF CHRIST
YOU WILL BE RAPTURED WITH HIM.
JESUS WAS WRAPPED
WHEN THEY LAID HIM IN A MANGER
WHERE THERE WAS NO ROOM FOR HIM IN THE INN.
HE WAS WRAPPED
WHEN THEY LAID HIM IN A BORROWED TOMB
THAT WASN'T THE END.
HE SHALL COME WRAPPED IN GLORY
WHEN HE COMES BACK AGAIN.
THE MORAL TO THIS STORY
IS TO BE WRAPPED IN HIM.
WHEN HE COMES AGAIN, YOU WILL
BE WRAPPED IN HIS GLORY
NOW YOU KNOW THE TRUE STORY.

Karen Jackson

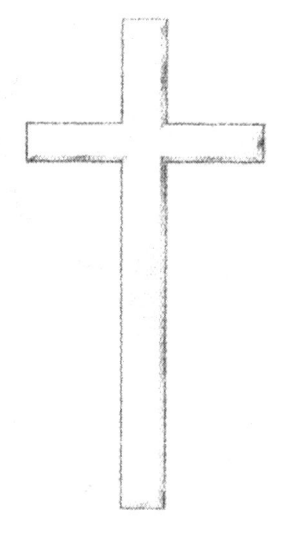

SAVIOR

THIS CHRISTMAS

LET JESUS

BECOME YOUR

SAVIOR, AND LIVE

WITH HIM FOREVER.

Karen Jackson

"I'LL RETURN"

THOU YOU SEE ME, IN A PAINTED GLASS

I'LL RETURN ONCE AGAIN

AND YOU'LL SEE ME AS I AM

THOU YOU SEE ME, IN A PAINTED GLASS

I'LL RETURN AT LAST, IN GLORY

AND MY STORY IS, WE WILL REIGN

TOGETHER AND FOREVER, PROCLAIMING THE

KINGDOM OF GOD.

WE FOREVER AND TOGETHER, WE WILL REIGN

WE'LL REIGN, WE'LL REIGN.

I'LL RETURN ONCE AGAIN, I'LL RETURN ONCE AGAIN,

ONCE AGAIN, ONCE AGAIN.